CONTENTS

WELCOME TO THE RAINFOREST

THE RAINFOREST HOME

Reptiles and amphibians are cold-blooded creatures that live both on land and in water. They can live in almost all regions of the Earth, but are well suited to the warmth and dampness of the tropics. Rainforests are found near the Equator, between the tropics of Cancer and Capricorn. Temperatures are high and rainfall is greater than 2,000 mm every year. Rainforests are found in parts of South and Central America, Africa, South-east Asia and Australasia. The rainforests are home to some of the world's most interesting and unusual reptiles and amphibians.

▼ A map showing the extent of the world's tropical rainforests today, compared with their coverage 500 years ago, before large-scale deforestation began.

▶ The warm, moist conditions found in the rainforests of the world provide amphibians such as this banana frog with ideal living conditions.

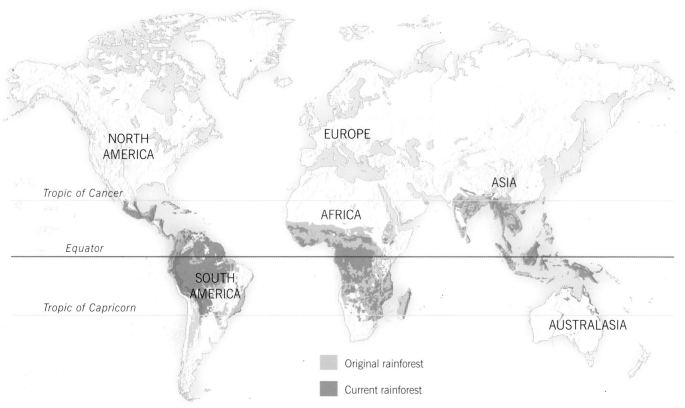

NORTH AMERICA

EUROPE

ASIA

Tropic of Cancer

AFRICA

Equator

SOUTH AMERICA

Tropic of Capricorn

AUSTRALASIA

Original rainforest

Current rainforest

Source: *World Conservation Monitoring Centre*

▲ Snakes are reptiles that slither through the vegetation. This red-tailed racer from South-east Asia is typical of snakes commonly found in the world's rainforests.

REPTILES AND AMPHIBIANS OF THE AMAZON RAINFOREST

The Amazon region of South America is the largest area of continuous rainforest on Earth. In the Amazon giant snakes up to 9 m long swim in the rivers and slither between the tall trees in search of prey. In the twilight world of the rainforest floor, brilliantly coloured poison-arrow frogs hop through the dead leaves that gather at the base of rainforest trees. High above the forest floor, cup-shaped plants called bromeliads collect water and provide homes for tadpoles and young frogs. Along the edges of rivers and in shallow lakes, huge caimans float like harmless logs before striking their prey with lightning speed.

This book will mainly focus on the reptiles and amphibians that live in the Amazon rainforest. Like all rainforests, the Amazon has special types of reptiles and amphibians that do not exist anywhere else in the world.

There are many species of amphibians and reptiles that have evolved to live in the cooler conditions of the tropical montane forests.

A view of part of the Amazon rainforest, which is a lowland forest. It is home to thousands of species of amphibians and reptiles.

TYPES OF RAINFOREST

Tropical rainforests can be divided into two main types, according to their height above sea level. These are lowland forest and tropical montane forest. Lowland forests are the most widespread stretches of rainforest and contain the majority of rainforest reptiles and amphibians. Tropical montane forest occurs in the tropics on hills and mountains above 900 m, where conditions are generally cooler. The trees in tropical montane forests are typically shorter than lowland forests and are often hidden in dense mists, which has given rise to their alternative name, 'cloud forests'. Tropical montane forests are home to their own species of reptiles and amphibians, such as the smoky mountain frog, which lives in Central America.

Fascinating Fact

Some species of frogs in Madagascar are adapting to other habitats as their natural home is lost through deforestation.

THE SPECTACLED CAIMAN

Caimans are found in Central and South America. Their habitat ranges from southern Mexico to Brazil. The spectacled caiman (see right) is recognized by the bony ridge between its eyes, which is like the nose-bridge on a pair of spectacles. It is the most common species of caiman – more common than the yellow caiman or the black caiman, which both share the same habitat.

All caimans feed on fish. They also eat deer and tapirs and sometimes feed on birds. Occasionally they will eat other caimans. They are fearsome predators and top of the food chain. They hunt by stealth, often lying completely still below the surface of the water, with just their eyes and nostrils visible, waiting to take their prey by surprise.

Spectacled caimans have bony deposits on their bodies, rather like an armour plating. This makes their skins difficult to sell. For this reason spectacled caimans have not been hunted as heavily as the black and yellow species, which share the same habitats.

THE IMPORTANCE OF REPTILES AND AMPHIBIANS

Reptiles and amphibians play an important part in the rainforest ecosystem. The role of frogs, for example, is vital in the rainforest food chain because they eat insects. In this way frogs control the number of insects, but they also provide a source of food for fish, mammals, reptiles, birds and large insects and spiders. Snakes and lizards are the main source of food for some species of birds such as the snake-eating eagle and mammals such as the mongoose. The eggs of turtles are an important source of food for mammals and birds, as are the young soft-shelled hatchlings. Caimans control the number of piranhas in Amazonian rivers but small species of caiman also provide occasional food for the world's largest snake, the anaconda.

WHAT IS AN AMPHIBIAN?

An amphibian is a partly-aquatic animal, such as a frog, toad, salamander or newt. The word 'amphibian' comes from the Latin words 'amphi' and 'bios' meaning 'double life'. This refers to the way amphibians spend the first part of their lives in water and their adult lives on dry land. Almost all amphibians follow this sequence. Frogs, for example, begin life as larvae (tadpoles) after hatching underwater from soft eggs, and breathe through their gills. As they grow, they start to change from tadpoles into miniature frogs. After a few weeks, their tail has gone, and four legs and lungs have developed to replace their gills. When they are fully grown, amphibians live on dry land, but they often still enter the water, mainly to breed. Amphibians gain and lose water through their skins so they must keep themselves moist.

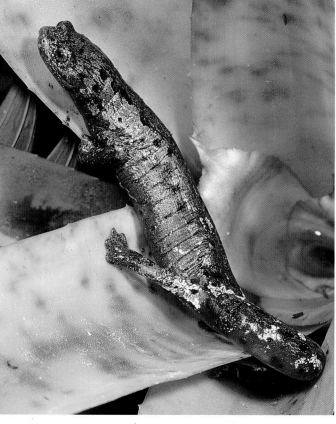

▲ Salamanders, like this bromeliad salamander from Guatemala, are one of four main types of rainforest amphibians.

WHAT IS A REPTILE?

A reptile is a scaly skinned creature, such as a lizard, snake, turtle, tortoise, alligator or crocodile. The easiest way of telling the difference between a reptile and an amphibian is by touching them. The skin of reptiles is dry rather than moist, and tough to protect them from attack and against water loss.

Like amphibians, reptiles also lay eggs, but on land, so their young are not raised in the water. An egg with a fluid-filled sac (called an amniotic sac) around the embryo provides nourishment for the baby reptile and the egg's hard shell protects it from attack. A miniature adult

Fascinating Fact

Some rainforest snakes have evolved on separate continents, thousands of kilometres apart, yet they are almost identical.

THE PYGMY MARSUPIAL FROG

Most frogs and toads lay their eggs in water where they remain until they hatch. Some frogs and toads, however, have developed unusual ways of caring for their eggs.

One group of frogs is known as the marsupial frogs because the females have a special sac on their back for their eggs. The pygmy marsupial frog comes from Venezuela. After the male pygmy marsupial frog has mated with the female, she produces eggs. The male then places the eggs in the sac on the female's back where they are kept moist, rather like being in water. The eggs develop into tadpoles in the sac. When they are a few weeks old, the female releases her tadpoles (see left) into a pool of water to complete their development from tadpoles into frogs.

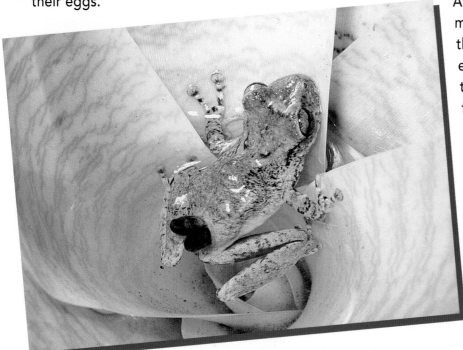

emerges from the egg and can begin a life similar to an adult's straight away. Reptiles are less dependent on water than amphibians, but spend their lives partly in water and partly on dry land.

As a young reptile grows bigger, it sheds its skin to reveal a new skin underneath. Reptiles continue to grow and shed their skins throughout their lives.

▶ The dry, scaly skin of this anaconda snake from the Amazon rainforest is typical of the skin of a reptile.

KEEPING A REGULAR TEMPERATURE

A warm-blooded creature, such as a mammal or a bird, is able to maintain a fairly constant body temperature, even when it is hot or cold in their environment. To do this, they eat frequently to provide the energy necessary to maintain this regular level. Because reptiles and amphibians are cold-blooded, however, they cannot keep their body temperature at a constant temperature. Instead, they are affected by the temperature of their surroundings. Reptiles and amphibians have to try to maintain a constant temperature level by moving in and out of sunlight, shade or water. They move between these hot and cooler places in order to avoid getting too hot or too cold so that their body organs can function well.

▲ An Amazonian lizard basks in a patch of sunlight on the forest floor in order to warm itself up.

▼ Cold-blooded reptiles such as caimans eat far less often than warm-blooded mammals or birds.

THE AMAZONIAN RIVER TURTLE

After a cool night, this species of Amazonian river turtle will climb on to a log to warm up. It extends its neck and feet as far as possible to catch as much warmth as it can. Gradually, the turtle's body temperature begins to rise until it reaches a point at which all the internal organs of the body are functioning well. The turtle may then plunge into the water to look for food. After a while in the cool water, the turtle's body temperature begins to drop.

The turtle finds another log on which to bask. The turtle repeats the process of warming up and cooling down several times a day.

The advantage of not having to use energy to maintain their body temperatures is that reptiles can live on very little food – a snake, for example, needs only $1/10$th to $1/100$th of the food required for a mammal or bird of the same weight.

KEEPING WARM AND COOLING DOWN

Rainforests are ideal environments for amphibians and reptiles because they maintain fairly constant temperatures. After a cool night, however, reptiles and amphibians need to get warm and they usually do this by lying in the sun.

Many reptiles and amphibians turn a darker colour in order to absorb the sun's warmth better. Once they are warm enough, their bodies become more active and they may look for food. When they need to cool down, some species of reptiles and amphibians become paler to reflect the heat. They may take a dip in the water, or crawl into the shade of the rainforest, emerging only in the cool of the evening. At night, reptiles and amphibians usually sleep, but some small species of lizards (called geckos) including the New Caledonian crested gecko and snakes such as the West African night adder, are active on warm nights.

THE RANGE OF AMPHIBIANS AND REPTILES

Amphibians appeared on Earth around 370 million years ago and were descended from a group of lobe-finned bony fish. Reptiles evolved from amphibians around 315 million years ago and went on to develop into hundreds of different types of animals. These included the dinosaurs that dominated life on Earth for millions of years. Of the 20 different groups or orders of reptiles that existed in prehistoric times, only five exist today. Just four of these orders are found in the rainforests.

GROUPS OF AMPHIBIANS AND REPTILES

There are believed to be around 4,200 species of amphibians and 6,400 species of reptiles living in the world today.

▼ *Many reptiles, such as this sail-finned lizard resemble the dinosaurs.*

RAINFOREST SECRETS

THE AGE OF THE DINOSAURS

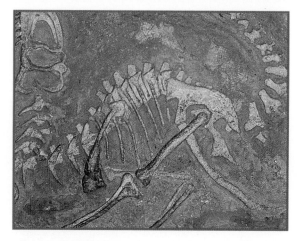

This is the fossil of an allosaurus, which was a fierce carnivorous reptile, 10.4 m in length. It existed when the dinosaurs dominated the planet about 220 million years ago. The 'age of the dinosaurs' lasted for more than 160 million years before they became extinct. So far, fossils of more than 500 different species have been unearthed but there were probably hundreds more which have not yet been discovered.

No one is exactly sure why the dinosaurs died out or why the types of reptile that exist today survived. Dinosaurs may have become extinct because of a drop in temperature. Small aquatic reptiles could have survived because the temperature of fresh water in lakes and streams does not vary as greatly as temperatures on land. In addition, small reptiles on land could warm up more quickly than the giant dinosaurs and were more likely to survive.

▲ The chameleon is a slow-moving lizard that lives in trees. Chameleons are found mainly in Africa and Madagascar.

▼ This yellow caiman is part of the order of crocodilians, which includes alligators and crocodiles.

The rainforests are believed to contain around two-thirds of all these species of reptiles and amphibians. Rainforest varieties range from saltwater crocodiles weighing more than 950 kg to miniature Amazonian lizards weighing just a few grammes.

Reptiles and amphibians can each be divided into different groups. Amphibians can be divided into three main groups or orders. Two of these groups – salamanders and newts, and frogs and toads – are all four-legged. But the third group of amphibians, which are called caecilians, have no legs at all. Their tubular, jointed bodies make them look rather like worms. Rainforest reptiles fall into four main groups or orders – lizards, snakes, turtles and tortoises, and crocodilians. The group of crocodilians includes alligators, crocodiles and caimans.

▼ *A typical frog that lives on the forest floor. It has smooth moist skin and long jumping legs. Its brown colour helps it to hide easily among dead leaves.*

FROGS AND TOADS

There are about 4,000 species of frogs and toads worldwide. The main difference between frogs and toads is based on their appearance. Frogs often have smooth, moist skin and long jumping legs while toads have drier, warty skin and shorter jumping legs.

Many species of frogs and toads are found in the rainforests. Amazonian tree frogs, which weigh only a few grammes, are tiny compared with giant toads such as the goliath toad from Africa. This huge toad could measure over 300 mm in length and weigh up to 3.5 kg.

RAINFOREST SECRETS

THE GIANT TOAD

The giant toad, sometimes called the cane toad, is one of the largest toads in the world. It can measure 240 mm from one end to the other. It lives in many types of tropical habitat and feeds on a wide variety of food, including insects (particularly beetles), and mammals such as small rodents, opossums and small birds.

The giant toad protects itself by secreting poisonous chemicals through its skin, which are deadly to many mammal predators.

Giant toads can breed at any time of the year. The females can lay as many as 350,000 eggs each year in the water, although a large number of these are eaten by predators.

▲ Like many other species, this salamander from Costa Rica in Central America is brightly coloured to let predators know that it is poisonous.

▼ Caecilians, like this one from West Africa, are often confused with snakes or worms because of their cylindrical, legless bodies and their burrowing lifestyle.

SALAMANDERS AND NEWTS

There are about 360 species of salamanders and newts. However, it is likely that there are many more species living in the rainforests that we have not yet discovered. Most salamanders and newts are brightly coloured and about 100–150 mm long, but some of the largest species can be over one metre in length. Some species of salamander have no lungs, such as the tlaconete salamander that lives in the tropical montane forests of Central Mexico. It breathes through its moist skin.

CAECILIANS

There are about 160–170 species of caecilians and they all live in tropical climates. These unusual amphibians spend most of their lives underground. Their bodies are ideally suited for burrowing under the soil. They also have thick skulls, and sunken eyes and mouth to avoid taking in too much earth as they burrow for worms and insects.

▼ *The green iguana of South and Central America is one of the most familiar types of rainforest lizard and is well suited to climbing among the trees.*

LIZARDS

There are an estimated 4,000 species of lizards worldwide – more than all the other types of reptiles combined. Many live in the rainforests. Lizards have long bodies covered with overlapping scales and most species have legs. Some lizards, such as chameleons, move very slowly and use their tail like a limb, to help them grip tree branches. Others, such as basilisk lizards, run fast on their two hind legs. The flying dragon can extend its wing-like flaps so it glides between trees, while the Madagascan day gecko has developed sticky pads on its toes to help it cling to flat surfaces.

RAINFOREST SECRETS

TOKAY GECKO LIZARD

The tokay gecko is a brightly coloured lizard from South-east Asia. Like all geckos, it has many miniature suction pads on its toes to help it walk along smooth, flat surfaces. It eats insects, such as flies and cockroaches, which it catches using its long, sticky tongue.

The rainforest habitat of the tokay gecko has been greatly reduced as rainforests have been turned into agricultural land and towns and cities have expanded. However, the tokay gecko has adapted to living in houses. Its special toes mean that it can hunt upside down on the ceiling of homes. Because the tokay gecko hunts insect pests, most people tolerate them living in their environment.

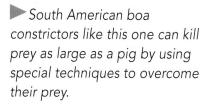
South American boa constrictors like this one can kill prey as large as a pig by using special techniques to overcome their prey.

Fascinating Fact

Snakes hunt by sight, sound and smell. They have no ears but they pick up vibrations from the ground and can smell with their tongue.

SNAKES

Snakes are reptiles that do not have limbs. There are around 2,500 species of snakes, but the largest and some of the most colourful are found in rainforests. The boa constrictor from the Amazon rainforest, for example, can reach lengths of 9 m, while an adult brahimy blind snake from South-east Asia grows to only 110 mm long. The range of colours and patterns varies, from the well camouflaged tree snake such as the red-tailed racer, to the brightly coloured red, black and yellow-banded coral snake.

Snakes have different ways of catching and killing their prey, but they usually swallow it whole. Snakes have evolved elasticated tendons on their jaws, which allows them to open their jaws very wide to swallow food that is much larger than the snakes themselves.

▼ *Turtles, such as this species of Amazonian river turtle, are excellent swimmers and spend most of their lives in or near the water.*

▼ *Tortoises, such as this species of African tortoise, spend their entire lives on dry land and forage among the leaf litter on the forest floor.*

TURTLES AND TORTOISES

Turtles and tortoises have existed in roughly the same form for more than 200 million years. Today, there are around 250 species of turtles and tortoises, mainly living in rivers in the tropical rainforests. Turtles and tortoises have soft bodies, which are protected inside a hard bony shell. They do not have teeth but bite with a horny beak that covers their mouth.

Turtles and tortoises have adapted to their rainforest environments in different ways.

RAINFOREST SECRETS

THE MATAMATA TURTLE

Matamata turtles are found in dark-water rivers and stagnant pools in the South American countries of Brazil, Colombia and Venezuela. The matamata turtle is one of the most curious-looking of all turtles. It is one of a number of species of turtle that have long, slender noses, which they use like snorkels to remain hidden underwater. The matamata is well camouflaged with a rough, ridged shell that looks like a piece of tree bark. It has a flattened head with loose flaps of skin that resemble the colour and shape of fallen leaves.

Matamata turtles feed on small fish, which are fooled by their camouflage. When the fish swim close to the turtle's mouth, they are gulped down.

Turtles are often aquatic while tortoises usually live on land. There is a huge variety in both size and pattern. Leatherback turtles can reach sizes of over 2 m in length, while Amazonian axe turtles can be as small as 140 mm long when they are fully grown.

CROCODILIANS

Crocodilians are a group of 22 reptile species. These are very large reptiles that have bony plates, like armour, along their backs. Crocodilians usually have long tails and short legs. Their mouths are made up of huge, powerful jaws, lined with sharp teeth.

The crocodilian group includes the largest reptiles alive today. Some can grow to 7 m in length and weigh nearly 1,000 kg. Crocodilians are powerful swimmers but tend to be ungainly on land. As they spend most of their time in the water, crocodilians have eyes and nostrils set high on their heads to remain above the water while the rest of the animal is submerged. They are all carnivorous predators and lie in wait for their prey.

The main differences between crocodiles and alligators (including caimans) are the width of their snouts and their number of teeth. Alligators have wider, more rounded snouts than crocodiles, which are thinner and squarer. Crocodiles have an extra tooth on each side of the lower jaw, visible when the jaw is closed.

▲ The spectacled caiman has powerful jaws and eyes set high on its head. This means it can float almost completely hidden underwater and still watch for unsuspecting prey.

TYPES OF RAINFOREST

Rainforests found in different parts of the world often look quite similar to each other. However, each is unique and contains different combinations of reptiles and amphibians.

Scientists recognize more than forty different types of rainforest. The most widespread type of rainforest is the lowland forest, which includes the Amazon rainforest in Brazil. Here the main division is between *terra firme* (dry ground forest) and *várzea* (flooded forest), which is underwater for several months of each year. Along about a quarter of tropical coastlines of lowland forests lie mangrove forests, another important type of rainforest. The higher tropical montane forests are cooler and wetter than the lowland forests.

▲ *A small Amazonian iguanid clings to the roots of a rainforest fig tree in the flooded forest (várzea) of the Amazon in Brazil.*

◀ *Rivers, lakes and even pools in the hollows of trees provide an ideal habitat for thousands of species of rainforest reptiles and amphibians.*

LAYERS OF THE RAINFOREST

There are varied habitats in each of the different layers of rainforest, from the canopy through to the rainforest floor. Some species of lizards, such as the many types of Amazonian iguanids, can move from the rainforest floor through the understorey and intermediate layers and even bask in the tropical sunshine in the emergent trees above the canopy.

Others such as the many species of tree frogs can live out their entire lives in a single bromeliad plant, high in the canopy. Tree snakes slither through the middle layers of rainforest where they can locate their prey with their heat sensors. Tortoises live on the forest floor, while the moist tropical soils provide a home for caecilians. Rivers and lakes are excellent habitats for species of turtles, crocodilians and aquatic snakes.

▼ *Snakes and iguanas can often be seen on the tallest trees basking in the sun to get warm.*

POOLS IN THE SKY

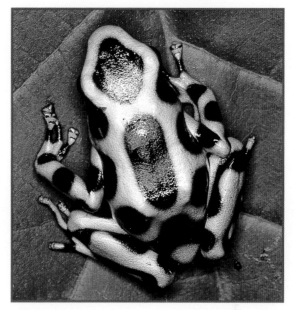

Tree frogs live high up in the canopy of rainforest trees. When they want to breed, some frogs slowly make their way down the tree trunks to rainforest pools. Their long legs and sticky toe pads help them to climb downwards.

Smaller tree frogs may spend their entire lives in the canopy. When these tree frogs breed, their tadpoles need to spend the early part of their lives in water. In many rainforests of South and Central America, bromeliads grow on the branches and trunks of trees high in the canopy. The leaves of the bromeliads form a rosette in the centre of the plant, which collects water. It is in these 'pools in the sky' that frogs such as the strawberry poison-arrow frog release their tadpoles, which they have carried on their backs since hatching. The strawberry poison-arrow frog is unusual because it feeds its young with eggs that never hatched.

MANGROVE FOREST

Mangrove forest grows on mud at the edges of seas and rivers. It is home to many reptiles and amphibians, such as the saltwater crocodile of northern Australia and the mangrove pit viper of Asia. There are a number of different types of mangrove forest around the world, covering an area of about 2,400 sq km, similar to the size of the state of California. Sea snakes, lizards and green turtles hunt for small insects, crustaceans and small fish among the bell-shaped roots of mangrove trees.

▲ Mangrove forest, such as this one in Tanzania, lines about a quarter of the world's tropical coastlines.

► Mangroves are home to some very rare reptiles and amphibians such as the mangrove pit viper.

MADAGASCAN TREE BOA

Despite its name, the Madagascan tree boa spends as much time on the forest floor as it does in the trees of the tropical montane forests of eastern Madagascar. Because tropical montane forest is cooler than lowland forest, this tree snake is often seen on the forest floor where it is either basking in the sun to warm up, or digesting its last meal. The tree boa is the smallest and most commonly-found boa on Madagascar. Tree boas are usually olive green and black with a shiny blue sheen, except for the young snakes, which are bright orange and red.

The Madagascan tree boa feeds mainly on warm-blooded prey.

The snake kills its prey by winding its body around it to strangle it, then swallowing it whole. The boa has a row of heat-sensitive sensors around its lips to help locate its warm-blooded prey in the dark.

▼ A chameleon sits and waits in a tree in Madagascar's tropical montane forest.

TROPICAL MONTANE FOREST

There are many species of reptiles and amphibians that have adapted to live in the cooler conditions of the tropical montane forests. Tropical montane forest is found in South American countries such as Venezuela and Colombia, Irian Jaya in Asia and Rwanda in Africa. Tropical montane forest trees are covered in many types of epiphytes – plants that grow on the trunks and branches. These plants, including orchids and bromeliads, are home to many types of insects, providing a source of food for frogs, lizards and tree snakes. Some species of reptiles and amphibians can be found as high as 4,000 m where trees are stunted and temperatures are only slightly above freezing.

PREDATORS

All adult amphibians and most reptiles are predators – they catch and eat other animals. Reptiles and amphibians can survive for long periods without food if necessary. A large crocodile or snake can sometimes go for several weeks or even months between meals. While some reptiles and amphibians eat almost anything they can catch, most species have very specific diets.

CARNIVOROUS AMPHIBIANS

All adult amphibians are carnivorous. Their diet includes insects, reptiles, small mammals and fish, but they have only a few ways of catching their prey. The most common method for frogs, toads, salamanders and newts is the use of a long, prehensile tongue with a sticky end.

▲ The skink is a reptile that feeds mainly on insects. All skinks have short limbs, and some may have a prehensile tail.

▼ This small lizard lives in the Amazon rainforest and preys mainly on insects.

MADAGASCAN CHAMELEONS

A chameleon is an expert insect hunter. It moves slowly through the rainforest with a rocking motion, waiting for an unsuspecting insect to draw near. When an insect is close, the chameleon flicks out its sticky tongue at lightning speed and captures the insect by dragging it into its mouth.

Over half of all the 135 species of chameleon that are known to exist are found in Madagascar. They are perfectly adapted to living in trees and usually have thin bodies to help them move between the tangle of branches, twigs and thorns. Their clamp-like feet give them a good hold on small branches. Most chameleons are greenish in colour but many can change their colour and patterning to hide amongst the leaves.

Chameleons have the unusual ability to move their eyes independently of each other, which allows them to look around while remaining motionless in a tree.

However, both eyes focus together when the chameleon spots its prey so that it can accurately land its sticky tongue on the insect, which it eats in an instant.

This is aimed at the prey with explosive speed. The victim enters the open mouth as the tongue recoils. The other way of catching food is by gulping it into a large mouth. Large amphibians such as the African bullfrog use this method to catch small mammals. Aquatic amphibians also catch prey that live in water by this technique. Like all amphibians, caecilians are toothless, and swallow their prey whole.

CARNIVOROUS REPTILES

Most reptiles are carnivorous. They have evolved a number of different methods for catching prey. A few lizards use their long, sticky tongue in the same way as amphibians, but most do not. Some snakes can catch a victim either with their fangs or with their sharp teeth.

◀ *The rows of teeth of this yellow caiman indicate that it is a carnivorous predator.*

RAINFOREST SECRETS

THE EYELASH VIPER

One of the most beautiful and deadly predators of South and Central America is the eyelash viper. Eyelash vipers are typically small, growing to lengths of between 400–600 mm. They belong to the most advanced group of venomous snakes – the pit vipers. This means that they have special folding, tubular fangs set at the front of the mouth to inject their deadly venom.

Pit vipers are usually nocturnal and feed on frogs, lizards, birds and small mammals. They have a wide range of colours and patterning from a uniform brown to brilliant yellow, red, green or grey with contrasting spots. They are superb predators and are well camouflaged on the flowers and fruits of a number of rainforest plants. They are so quick that they can strike even at fast-moving prey. This eyelash viper (see right) is lying in wait for a hummingbird to arrive and feed at the heliconia plant.

Others immobilize a victim with a venomous bite. Some snakes crush the air out of their prey until it has suffocated. Crocodiles and alligators usually drown their victims. They often let their prey partly decompose underwater, before tearing it into bite-size pieces by seizing it in their jaws and spinning rapidly in the water.

▲ There are two different species of Amazonian river turtle sitting on this log. They both eat mainly plant material and only occasionally feed on insects and small fish.

HERBIVORES AND OMNIVORES

There are only a few reptiles and a small number of species of lizards, turtles and tortoises that are herbivores. The largest of these are the green iguanas, which can grow to almost 2 m in length, and have a diet of mainly leaves and fruit. Other species of lizards such as the the rhinoceros iguana, live on seaweed alone. There are also types of land-living tortoises that are herbivores. Most reptiles are omnivores, however, and eat insects, slugs and fish in addition to plant material. This includes many species of lizards, turtles and tortoises. Different species of the South American river turtle eat mainly plants but may occasionally supplement their diet with other foods.

CAMOUFLAGE

Many species of amphibians and reptiles can blend into the rainforest background. Amazonian frogs, which hop along the forest floor, are similar in colour and shape to fallen leaves. The colours of the fringed geckos of Madagascar resemble the patterning of the bark of the trees they usually live on. Even large lizards such as the green iguanas, which are about a metre long, are difficult to see because their green bodies match the surrounding foliage. Many tree snakes are green so they can hide themselves away in the rainforest. Most frogs and toads also have the ability to change their colour to help them remain camouflaged. Tree frogs, including White's tree frog, can be dark brown or green when on the bark of a tree and pale leaf-green when they are amongst the foliage.

▲ An Amazonian lizard blends in almost perfectly with its background because of its speckled camouflage colours.

◄ Some rainforest frogs are not only the same colour as the background leaves they hide among but their shape is the same as those of the leaves.

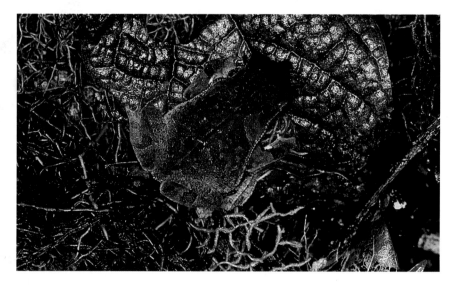

POISONS

Many types of frogs and salamanders are brilliantly coloured to advertise the fact that they are poisonous. This warns a predator that it could die a painful death if it tried

Fascinating Fact

A minute amount of poison from a poison-arrow frog could kill a mammal as large as a jaguar.

to eat one of these amphibians. Poison-arrow frogs secrete poisons through their skin while the giant toad has poison glands on its back, which it uses to squirt poison at its attacker. Some salamanders have poison glands on their heads and they swing their heads around wildly, trying to headbutt and poison their attacker. Some newts have poison glands in their tails and whip their attacker with it to defend themselves.

Some snakes and lizards produce foul-tasting liquids as a deterrent against predators that may try and eat them.

▲ *The brightly coloured coral snake is one of the most poisonous snakes in the world.*

RAINFOREST SECRETS

THE POISON-ARROW FROG

This poison-arrow frog from the Amazon has beautiful, colourful markings (see left). The colours tell predators that these small frogs are deadly poisonous. The Kokoi poison-arrow frog of Colombia, for example, can produce a poison that can be absorbed through the skin of a predator. Only $1/10{,}000$th of a gramme is enough to kill a human being. Indigenous people in South and Central America use the poisonous secretions from local species of poison-arrow frog to tip their blow-pipe darts and arrows when hunting. It is from this hunting activity that the poison-arrow frog got its name.

PROTECTIVE BODIES

Many reptiles have developed special shells or scales to help protect them from attack. Tortoises and turtles, for example, have a hard shell. When threatened, they can withdraw their head and legs into their shells, out of danger. Many crocodilians have armoured, bony scales along their backs to protect themselves from attack, often from larger individuals of the same species. Large lizards, such as sail-finned lizards or iguanas often display a ridge of bony, and sometimes sharp, scales along their backs.

The skin of all reptiles is impermeable, which means they do not lose water through their skin as amphibians do. The tough, scaly skins of snakes not only help to to keep in water but also protect the snake from attack. However, these skins are shed to permit the snake to grow. When a snake is young it will shed its skin more often as it grows more rapidly.

▲ *Like land-living tortoises, these turtles run the greatest risk of attack by predators during the first few weeks of their lives when their shells are still soft.*

Fascinating Fact
Some species of lizard have a tail that breaks off when it is grabbed by a predator. These lizards also have the ability to grow a new one.

THE BASILISK

This striking lizard usually lives in the tangled plants at the edges of streams in parts of Central America. It eats insects, snails and small fish and relies on camouflage both for hunting and for avoiding predators.

When threatened the basilisk has a very special means of escape. It rears up on its back legs and runs away at remarkable speed. It can run very fast on the ground, but it can also run away over water – on its webbed hind feet.

It is thought that the lizard is kept afloat by its speed, while its long tail helps it to keep its balance.

MAKING A SWIFT ESCAPE

Reptiles and amphibians are experts at jumping away from danger. Frogs regularly avoid attack by making large leaps powered by their muscular back legs. Flying frogs glide through the air, stopping their fall with their webbed feet and hanging on to branches with their sticky pads. Crocodiles, alligators and snakes can all move fast over short distances. Lizards can make fast getaways, sprinting out of danger on their back legs.

This rhinoceros iguana is about a metre long. If it is threatened by a predator it can move very quickly on its strong legs, despite its large size.

31

WHY ARE REPTILES AND AMPHIBIANS DISAPPEARING?

The number of many species of rainforest reptiles and amphibians has declined rapidly over the last twenty years. The golden toad from Costa Rica, for example, is thought to be extinct. Tree frogs, spectacled cobras, black caimans, and leatherback turtles have all declined and are now under threat.

▲ A golden toad from Costa Rica. Golden toads were once considered common. Twenty years later they are now thought to have become extinct because of changes in their environment.

The largest single cause for the decline of reptiles and amphibians is the destruction of their habitat. They are also sensitive to changes in environmental conditions, caused by pollution. They are vulnerable to changes in the local climate caused by global warming, which is the result of human activity through industrial processes.

Fascinating Fact

Scientists believe that chemicals that cause pollution are stopping many rare species from being able to breed properly.

◀ In the Amazon rainforest tortoises are often trapped by local people for food.

▲ The capture of many reptiles, including iguanas, for pets, has drastically reduced their numbers in the wild.

THE PET TRADE

Many species of reptiles are also caught for the pet trade. Rare species of animals can be worth tens of thousands of dollars in trade around the world. Every year, many thousands of rainforest amphibians and reptiles are caught for the international pet trade. Chinese water dragons (a type of lizard), boa constrictors, rare tree frogs and many other rainforest reptiles and amphibians are being sold in ever-increasing numbers. Large reptiles, such as iguanas and Amazonian caimans, are being offered today as pets in many of the world's richer countries.

LINKS

White's tree frog

White's tree frog comes from the rainforests of Australasia. This dumpy tree frog has become a popular pet. It changes colour as it moves from leaves on to tree trunks or onto the ground, which makes it very appealing. It is also popular because it is friendly, and can become tame. Some frogs can be trained to feed from the hand of their owner.

However, the popularity of the frog as a pet in the homes of people in North America and Europe has led to a massive decline in the numbers in the wild. White's tree frogs are protected by international law and are now officially protected in the rainforests of Australia. Frogs bred in captivity are now supplying the demand of pet stores, helping to keep up the numbers of this species of tree frog in the rainforests.

HUNTING FOR FOOD

Many indigenous peoples in the tropical rainforests have hunted reptiles and amphibians for food for thousands of years. The smoky mountain frog is known as 'the chicken of the forest' and is a regular part of some rainforest people's diet in Central America. Reptiles such as green iguanas also form an important part of people's diet. Over the last century millions of settlers have moved into rainforests and now some reptile species, such as the green iguana are threatened. Some species of Amazonian river turtles, which once lined the main rivers in their millions, have now been hunted almost to extinction in large parts of the rainforest. In parts of the world, such as the Far East, snake meat and turtle eggs are popular foods.

▲ The smoky mountain frog is commonly eaten by people who live in Central American countries such as Panama.

◀ Children helping to roast the turtles that their father has caught during the night in an Amazon settlement near Manaus, Brazil.

LINKS

Iguana Project

After years of hunting and with the demand for its meat increasing, the green iguana is in danger of becoming extinct in many areas. Special projects in Panama, Costa Rica and Mexico have been started where farmers have been encouraged to breed and 'farm' iguanas for food. Many small-scale farmers have taken up the scheme and now breed iguanas (see right). Iguanas can produce as much meat per hectare as cattle, but at a fraction of the cost. This scheme helps local people provide for themselves without over-hunting wild iguanas in the rainforest.

SKIN TRADE

The hunting of animals for their skins has caused reptile numbers to decline in the rainforests. Spectacled cobras from Thailand, boa constrictors and caimans from South America, and many other types of reptiles have very valuable skins, and have been hunted heavily. The rarer the skin of the reptile, the more people will be prepared to pay for it. Killing endangered reptiles continues, even though it is often illegal to do so. For poor people in the rainforest, selling skins is one way to earn money to feed their families. On a bigger scale, criminal organizations often smuggle skins to wealthy buyers in the rich countries of the world.

◀ Caiman skins are valuable and caimans are often hunted to increase a family's income.

DISAPPEARING HABITATS

The tropical rainforests have a greater variety of species of amphibians and reptiles than any other type of habitat. When they are destroyed, many species become extinct. Huge areas of rainforest are being cut down for commercial activities – timber, firewood, charcoal and wood pulp for paper. Vast areas are also being converted into agricultural land. Soya bean production in the Amazon rainforest, African oil palm plantations in West Africa and rice cultivation in Asia have caused the loss of millions of hectares of rainforest. Building dams and mines and the expansion of towns and cities have also led to rainforest loss. Not only are huge areas of rainforest being burned and destroyed, but areas of rainforest are also becoming fragmented. This makes it more difficult for animals such as turtles to migrate to their breeding grounds.

POLLUTION

Today, there are higher levels of pollution than ever before. Toxic gases are produced by factories and human and chemical waste is found in almost all the world's seas, rivers and lakes.

◀ *Large commercial operations such as mining have destroyed and polluted large areas of rainforest. This means that many local species of reptiles and amphibians no longer exist.*

▼ *The skin of all frogs is thin and is designed to absorb water and oxygen from the atmosphere. Frogs can die if pollution from the atmosphere is absorbed through their skin.*

Dangers to Leatherback Turtles

The leatherback turtle (see right) is the largest of all turtles, growing to over 2 m long and weighing more than 850 kg when fully grown. Many turtles nest on beaches near mangrove forests and hunt in the shallow coastal waters of rainforest islands. Different species of leatherback turtle can easily swim the width of the Atlantic or Pacific Oceans, which they do on their annual migrations.

Ocean-going turtles experience different dangers from those that live only in rainforest rivers and streams. Leatherbacks often get caught up and drown in the huge nets used to catch commercial fish, such as tuna at sea. They are also known to have died because they often mistake plastic bags for jellyfish. Excellent beaches often attract the development of holiday resorts, which displace the nesting turtles.

▼ Water-borne chemicals can easily pass through the skins of tadpoles and mean the tadpoles may not develop properly.

Amphibians are easily harmed by pollutants because their thin skins readily absorb chemicals from their surroundings. For example, mercury has been released into Amazonian rivers by gold miners in recent years. This can prevent tadpoles from forming normally as they grow. Pollutants can also poison fish, which, in turn, poison the reptiles that eat fish from the rivers. Similarly, reptiles and amphibians eat insects, which may have been in contact with DDT, a pesticide used to keep down the numbers of insects in the tropics. Nobody knows the long-term effects of DDT on reptiles and amphibians.

The habitats of many rare species of reptiles and amphibians are being lost as logging companies cut down the rainforests.

SAVING THE SPECIES

No one knows exactly by how much the wild populations of rainforest amphibians and reptiles have declined or how many species have become extinct. All that is certain is that without conservation projects the number of extinctions per year will continue to rise. Fortunately, there are many concerned individuals and environmental organizations that are fighting hard for a better future for reptiles and amphibians. By far the most serious problem is destruction of the rainforest. Many development and environmental organizations are campaigning hard to reduce the rate at which the world's rainforests are lost. Many rainforest communities are receiving education about how to find alternative employment for people working in the destructive industries of logging, cattle farming and hunting. Other problems are being tackled, such as hunting for skins and

In many countries such as Brazil there are park guards who help look after the rainforest.

Preventing Illegal Imports

At major international airports such as Heathrow in London there are specially trained customs officers. They try and prevent the import of endangered reptiles and other species. Every week customs officers may find anything from live turtles and snakes to items such as caiman skin handbags (see right).

Customs officers act under international laws set out under an agreement aimed at reducing the trade of rare and endangered species. Britain is one of the top three destinations in the world for both legal and illegal imports.

WWF-UK campaigns to highlight the problem of illegally imported goods.

Fascinating Fact

It is estimated that 100 million reptile skins are traded legally and illegally each year.

collecting animals for medicines. Environmental organizations are promoting international laws to protect rare species, and trying to reduce pollution.

PROTECTED AREAS

One of the ways of helping rare rainforest reptiles and amphibians to survive is to protect the rainforests in which they live. If the areas are large enough, many species of rare amphibians and reptiles can be given a good chance of survival. Organizations such as WWF have successfully campaigned for protected areas to be set up all over the world. These can take the form of national parks, nature reserves, community managed land, rainforest reserves, certified rainforest areas and rainforest corridors that link large areas of rainforest. There are very few areas specifically protected for amphibians and reptiles. However, if areas are set up to protect rare birds or mammals, this means that reptiles and amphibians can benefit as well.

RESEARCH

Conservation projects can only be effective if they are based on good research. The lives of many rainforest amphibians and reptiles are complicated. It can take researchers years to begin to understand an animal's role in an ecosystem and what needs to be done to protect it from becoming extinct.

Scientists carry out research to estimate the numbers of rare animals, and to study how the particular animals respond to changes in their habitats. For example, some rare species such as the egg-eating snakes rely on one specific type of food. Others require special habitats in order to reproduce, such as the tree frogs that lay their eggs in the water contained in bromeliad plants. By studying what some rare species need to survive, scientists can advise conservation organizations about the type of rainforest that needs to be protected and the action they should take.

▲ The breeding of turtles in captivity is one way of helping to restore numbers to an area of rainforest.

▼ Mucus from the back of the Brazilian bicoloured tree frog may be useful in medical research.

REPTILES FOR MEDICINE

Rainforest reptiles and amphibians are important in the research and development of medicines. The poisonous and foul-smelling secretions produced by frogs and toads have been shown to have many medical applications from painkillers to antibiotics.

Mamiraua – A Model for Conservation

The setting up of the Mamiraua ecological reserve in the state of Amazonas in Brazil in 1992 has provided a model for conservation in the Amazon. The reserve covers 1,124,000 hectares of flooded forest, creating a protected area where local people and wildlife live side by side.

In the reserve, the people live a traditional lifestyle, collecting rainforest fruits and seeds, fishing, and hunting animals such as turtles. However, the level of these activities is closely controlled so they do not damage the rainforest ecosystem. Mamiraua also has legal protection against poaching. The numbers of rare black caimans and Amazonian river turtles (see baby turtle, right) have been increasing ever since the setting up of the reserve.

The Brazilian bicoloured tree frog, for example, produces a special mucus that affects how well the nerve cells function. This may help in treating diseases to do with the brain or nervous system in humans. The venoms from many deadly snakes have also been shown to reduce high blood pressure and improve the consistency of a person's blood.

The chemicals that help some amphibians and reptiles to grow a limb or tail after being attacked are also being investigated for possible use in transplant surgery. Some snakes are captured and samples of their venom taken before they are released again. Chemists need only small amounts to work out the chemical structure of the active ingredient, which they can later manufacture themselves.

EDUCATION

Education is an important part of conservation. Large landowners often destroy the rainforest they own or drain important wetland and mangrove habitats for agriculture and ranching. With better education, they could cause far less damage and give themselves a better income. They could work in ecotourism, or collect sustainable products such as palm fruits and nuts. Many small rainforest communities can learn about ways of conserving rainforest resources in ways that do not harm the environment, and preserve it for the future.

▲ A sign for the national park in Madagascar, which was set up for the protection of all wildlife that lives within it.

Children of the Flooded Forest

These are children from the villages of San Juan and Aracampinas in the flooded forest near the Amazonian town of Santarem. They are learning about the local environment in their lessons at school. One of their practical projects arose from talking to the older members of their villages about what life was like fifty years ago. They discovered that there are very few turtles seen in the rivers today compared with only a few decades ago.

In 2000, the children decided to organize their own captive breeding project. Turtle eggs were collected from the local beaches and the turtles were raised until they were mature enough to look after themselves (see below). This scheme should lead to an increase in the numbers of turtles locally.

Organizations such as WWF and Friends of the Earth support many environmental education schemes in schools, in the hope that the next generation will be better informed about how to look after the natural world around them. They can learn about different species that live in the rainforests, such as snakes, so they can avoid unnecessary killing of harmless reptiles. Environmental education is also important for children in non-rainforest countries so that they are aware of what they can do to help save rare amphibians and reptiles from extinction.

INTERNATIONAL LAW

Over the last few decades, wildlife has been given much more protection by the introduction of new international and national laws. In many countries, there are laws that aim to stop the hunting of rare mammals. There are also special international laws to prevent all rare animal products and skins – including the skins of snakes and frogs – being traded around the world. The International Convention for the Trade in Endangered Species (CITES) is an agreement by which countries agree to help protect rare species from becoming extinct. CITES maintains a list of endangered amphibians and reptile species that are illegal to traffic. The law has been very successful for some rare species. The population of reptiles, such as the estuarine crocodile in Queensland, Australia has recovered so well that there are almost too many. The creeks close to the sea have now become dangerous for tourists.

▼ *The protection of the habitat of the estuarine crocodile in Australia has led to a huge increase in numbers.*

THE PROBLEMS

The future for rainforest reptiles and amphibians looks uncertain. The rainforests in which they live are being destroyed faster than ever before and other human activities are also pushing many reptile and amphibian species to the brink of extinction. Pollution of the rivers and lakes is causing a drastic decline in wild populations, and the introduction of alien species has also devastated local reptile and amphibian populations. Many reptiles and amphibians live in very specific conditions and if these trends continue, the only future for many species may well be in zoos and scientific institutions.

A POSITIVE RESPONSE

Fortunately, more and more people are taking an interest in protecting as many different species as possible. Environmental organizations such as WWF have been campaigning for the world's governments to

▲ *It is important that rare crocodilians are protected to ensure their survival in the future.*

▼ *Captive breeding and release into the wild may help increase the numbers of endangered reptiles and amphibians.*

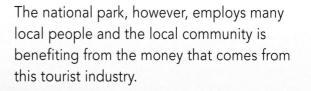

Ecotourism

Madagascar has thousands of unique species of reptiles and amphibians in its rainforests. Today, tourists are keen to pay to visit a rainforest to see unusual creatures. About 250 km from the capital of Madagascar is a national park. People come to visit the park from all over the world. They are not only interested in its population of lemurs, but also Madagascar's unique species of amphibians and reptiles. Chameleon tours are particularly popular with the tourists.

Around 95 per cent of Madagascar's rainforest has been destroyed and people have lost not only this habitat but also the opportunity to make a living from it.

The national park, however, employs many local people and the local community is benefiting from the money that comes from this tourist industry.

▼ This Amazonian tree frog sits camouflaged on a branch. It is a local species, not widely known, and is just one example of the variety of rainforest amphibians.

act responsibly in trying to develop rainforest areas. They encourage them to honour the United Nation's Convention on Biological Diversity, where nations are obliged to take action to protect its rarest species. Many indigenous people know that a balance is possible – and that people can inhabit and make a living from the rainforests without destroying the rainforests or the creatures that live in them.

People all around the world are becoming more aware that creatures, other than humans have a right to continue to exist on the planet. Reptiles and amphibians are not only part of the local ecosystem but also part of the rich variety of life on Earth.

GLOSSARY

aquatic An animal or plant that lives in or near water.

bromeliads A group of plants that have a rosette of spiny leaves.

camouflaged When the shape, colours or patterns of an animal help it to blend in with its surroundings.

canopy The layer of trees between the forest floor and the tallest towering treetops.

carnivorous Usually refers to an animal that feeds on the flesh or meat of other animals.

crustacean A hard-shelled animal such as a crab or lobster, that is usually aquatic.

decompose To rot, or to break down into component parts and chemicals.

ecological To do with the study of the inter-relationship between organisms and all aspects of their environment.

ecosystem The relationship of plants and living organisms to each other and the environment.

ecotourism Helping to conserve rainforests by encouraging tourists to visit.

food chain A series of living things, each of which is dependent on the next for food.

fossils The remains of plants or animals from hundreds of thousands of years ago, preserved in solid rock.

hatchlings Young creatures that have just emerged from eggs.

herbivore Usually refers to a creature that eats only plants.

migration The seasonal movement of living things from one location to another.

nocturnal Describes a creature that is active mainly at night.

pesticides Chemicals used to control pests, such as flies.

pollutants Materials that harm the environment.

prehensile Part of an animal's body that can grab or act like a limb.

prey An animal that is hunted and killed by another for food.

species A group of plants or animals that closely resemble one another.

thyroid A gland in the neck that produces hormones that affect development.

wetland An area of land that remains waterlogged for most of the year.

White's tree frog.

FURTHER INFORMATION

BOOKS TO READ

Closer Look at the Rainforest by Selina Wood (Franklin Watts, 1996)

Geography Detective: Rainforest by Philip Sauvain (Zöe Books, 1996)

Journey into the Rainforest by Tim Knight (Oxford University Press, 2001)

Jungle by Theresa Greenaway (Dorling Kindersley, 1994)

The Rainforest by Karen Liptak (Biosphere Press, 1993)

Secrets of the Rainforest by Michael Chinery (Cherrytree, 2001)

The Wayland Atlas of Rainforests by Anna Lewington (Hodder Wayland, 1996)

WEBSITES

There are many websites about the rainforests. Type in key words to search for the information you need, or visit the following sites:

Passport to the Rainforest
http://www.passporttoknowledge.com/rainforest/main.html
Includes maps, graphics, images and information about plants and animals.

Rainforest Action Network
http://www.ran.org/
Facts about rainforest people and animals presented in a question and answer format. Includes action that children can take to conserve the rainforests.

Rainforest Conservation Fund
http://www.conservation.org/
Provides species data for plants and animals including news, projects and articles.

Rainforest Information Centre
http://www.forests.org/ric/
News, information, ecology and conservation. Includes a links page for children.

Species Survival Network CITES Conference
http://www.defenders.org/cites.html
Information on CITES conferences, which discuss the world's endangered species. It includes appendixes of endangered animals and plants.

World Rainforest Movement
http://www.wrm.org.uy/
Includes information on rainforests by country and by subject.

WWF–UK
http://www.wwf.org.uk/
In addition to its main website in the UK, the environmental organization has a number of sites devoted to different campaigns.
http://www.panda.org/
The international site for WWF.
http://www.panda.org/forest4life
The forests for life campaign.

CD ROM

Rainforest (Interfact) by Lucy Baker and Jason Page (Two-Can, 1998)

VIDEO

The Decade of Destruction by Adrian Cowell (Central Independent Television, 1991)

ADDRESSES OF ORGANIZATIONS

Friends of the Earth, 26-28 Underwood Street, London N1 7JQ Tel: 020 7490 1555
http://www.foe.co.uk/
Greenpeace, Canonbury Villas, London N1 2PN
Tel: 0207 865 8100
http://www.greenpeace.org.uk/
Oxfam, Oxfam House, Banbury Road, Oxford, OX2 7DZ Tel: 01865 312610
http://www.oxfam.org.uk/
Survival International, 6 Charterhouse Buildings, London EC1M 7ET Tel: 020 7687 8700
http://www.survival-international.org/
WWF–UK, Panda House, Weyside Park, Godalming, Surrey GU7 1XR Tel: 01483 426444
http://www.wwf.org.uk/

INDEX

Picture acknowledgements:
All photographs are by Edward Parker with the exception of the following: Ecoscene 43 (W. Lawler); OSF 8 (Zig Leszczynski), 9 top (Michael Fogden), 15 top (Robert A. Lubeck/Animals/Animals), 15 bottom (J.A.L Cooke), 18 both (David M. Dennis), 26 bottom (Michael Fogden), 31 top (Joe McDonald Animals/ Animals), 32 top (Mike Linley/Survival Anglia), 40 (Paul Franklin); Papilio 14 bottom (Paul Franklin).